DIALOGUE WITH THE DIVINE

— PRAYERS AND MEDITATIONS —

HIS HOLINESS POPE SHENOUDA III
OF THRICE-BLESSED MEMORY

ST. MARY & MOSES ABBEY PRESS

Dialogue with the Divine: Prayers and Meditations
By His Holiness Pope Shenouda III of Thrice-Blessed Memory

Book Translation and Design (cover and interior) by:
St. Mary and St. Demiana Convent
330 Village Dr.
Dawsonville GA 30534
convent.suscopts.org

Published by:
St. Mary & St. Moses Abbey Press
101 S Vista Dr, Sandia, TX 78383
stmabbeypress.com

Library of Congress Control Number: 2022935201

Dialogue with the Divine: Prayers and Meditations
by His Holiness Pope Shenouda III
of Thrice-Blessed Memory

CONTENTS

Foreword by His Grace Bishop Youssef i

A Foreword on Prayer by His Holiness Pope Shenouda iii

MEDITATIONS
1.   You, O Lord, Alone 1
2.   O Lord, You Shepherd Me 2
3.   Who Am I, O Lord 4
4.   May Your Will Be Done 6
5.   I Want to Live With You 8
6.   Return Us, O Lord, That We May Return to You 9
7.   Leave Me Alone! 16
8.   You, and You Alone, O Lord 20
9.   I Want You, O Lord 21
10.   Grant the Spirit from Your Resources 24
11.   Out of the Depth of my Heart I Cried to You 25
12.   Let My Prayer Come Before You 27
13.   I Confess Before You, O Lord 30
14.   Come Lord and Reign, Behold I Am Yours 34
15.   Lord, Teach Me Humility 36
16.   Save Me, O Lord 38
17.   Draw Me Away! We Will Run After You 40
18.   O Lord, I Love You from My Depth 42
19.   Lord, I Have Many Things to Say 47
20.   You, O Lord, are Compassionate and Gentle 49
21.   Lord, I Cannot Find Any Besides You 50
22.   Lord, Of Your Own We Have Given You 51
23.   Let It Alone This Year Also 53
24.   Lord, You Are Beyond My Thoughts 55
25.   Your Kingdom Come 58
26.   Blessed Are You, O Lord 60
27.   Fulfill Your Promises to Us 61
28.   I Will Not Leave You 63
29.   Yes Lord, Yours Is the Power and the Glory 66
30.   Chasten Me O Lord 70
31.   To You, O Lord, Do I Complain 71
32.   Blessed Are You, O Lord 73
33.   You Are Life Itself 74
34.   Do Not Deprive Me Of Working With You 75

35.	You Are Inside Me	76
36.	I Want To Draw Closer To You	79
37.	You, O Lord, Exist	82
38.	I Thank You, O Lord	84
39.	Have Mercy On Me	85
40.	I Want To Forget Myself	86
41.	I Want Nothing From the World	87
42.	I Finally Found You	88

POETRY

A Whisper of Love	89
I Love You, O Lord	91
O My Lord	92

REFERENCES

93

Foreword

His Holiness Pope Shenouda III is a treasure chest. Oh, if one could peek inside! This book is exactly the vent through which we can peek into his soul. Here we taste the sweetness of his God-centered life through his dialogues with God. We cannot say that we can see the full scope of his intimate relationship with God, but for a moment, we can feel and share in his longing for unity with our Lord, speaking to Him from his heart, debating with Him, discussing with Him, and begging Him. This book certainly can teach a person how to pray—how to have dialogue with the Divine.

This book, originally compiled by St. Demiana Monastery in Egypt, was published under the title "Monaga." It is a compilation from His Holiness Pope Shenouda's various lectures and books, snatching up the moments of his deepest conversations with God. Here, St. Mary and St. Demiana Convent in Georgia has translated it into English. The translation is neither literal (rendering a rigid read), nor figurative (losing the intended meaning of his words). However, it is a comfortable medium, carrying the meaning and spirit of his words and simultaneously an enjoyable read for the fluent English speakers. All the credit goes to His Holiness' fluency in expressing himself, and any mistakes are to be blamed on us.

His Holiness Pope Shenouda III was the 117th Pope and Patriarch of the Coptic Orthodox Church of Alexandria. He was first ordained a monk at Saint Mary's Monastery, Natrun Desert, Egypt (known as Deir Al-Sourian), in 1954. He was chosen Patriarch of the Coptic Orthodox Church in 1971 and sat on the throne of the See of St. Mark for more than 40 years. He had begun holding weekly spiritual meetings since the 60s when he was ordained bishop, and so the contents of this book are gleaned from those meetings and his publications—over 50 years of intimate conversations with God.

We pray this book inspires the readers to a deeper relationship with the Divine.

His Grace Bishop Youssef
Bishop of the Coptic Orthodox Diocese
of the Southern United States
Commencement of the Ninevites Fast
February 14, 2022

A FOREWORD ON PRAYER

Prayer is the Pleasure of the Spirit
By His Holiness Pope Shenouda III

The life of love and companionship with God is a Holy of Holies, worthy of silence. How deep are the feelings that stem from being in the presence of God, how plenteous they are! Just the sense of being with God lifts one up to a level higher than this world, more excellent than any material value, and all feelings become spiritual—deep.

The heart is drawn to God, and clings to Him in love. It sees its joy in attaching to Him, singing with David the Prophet, "it is good for me to draw near to God" (Ps 73:28). The heart wishes to continue towards God, and always yearns to go in that direction. Rejoicing to have found God, the soul cleaves to Him, chanting with the Shulamite, "I held him and would not let him go" (Song 3:4). With a longing for life to remain here, in this encounter with God and a sense of His presence, all other desires become trivial.

When in union with the Lord, you are unable to tear yourself away from this spiritual delicacy you have found in the Lord, crying out from the depths with St. Paul: "Who shall separate us from the love of Christ? Shall tribulation, or distress, or persecution, or famine, or nakedness, or peril, or sword? Neither death nor life, nor angels nor principalities nor powers, nor things present nor things to come, nor height nor depth, nor any other created thing, shall be able to separate us from the love of God which is in Christ Jesus" (Rom 8:35, 38-39). Can you say this, and not allow anything to separate you from being with God?

The saints' biographies tell of one monk who was walking in the wilderness, absorbed in prayer with all his heart and his emotions. When two angels came and walked along with him, he would not allow himself to leave his prayer to look to either one of them, but continued in his prayers and meditations, saying: "Who shall separate us from the love of Christ?... I am persuaded... neither death nor life, nor angels nor principalities nor powers, nor things present nor things to come" (Rom 8:35, 38).

The feelings of being with God are inexpressible; you feel them. If you try to describe them, you cannot. At times, it reaches a point where a person is dazzled and amazed. Reawakening, one is filled with overwhelming joy, and feels an inclination towards silence, not wanting to come down from these inmost feelings to the level of talking with people.

Among these feelings are love, joy, and peace—fruits of the Holy Spirit—who (along with His fruits) dwells in the human heart at times of being with God. This is being with God—love in Love; a simple love meets with infinite Love. A human heart comes into contact with God; a limited heart comes in contact with the Unlimited Heart. We, in our lives with God, are as a simple creek which runs until it meets the Sea, and pours into it, and blends with its endless waters. We are a drop of water, heated by the fervor of love, which evaporates, and so rises in order to come down into the depths of the Great River. Our life with God is a life of love.

Beloved, it is enough for you to meet with Christ, to talk with Him, to listen to Him, to create a relationship with Him, finding all your necessities in Him, not needing anything but to be with Him, to give Him your heart, then you will feel the ridiculousness of the whole world, and will delight in God's love.[1]

If you want to love God, take Him for a friend. Rather, let Him be your best friend, the one you rush to, before anyone else. Reveal your secrets to Him, tell Him everything, feel the deepest comfort in being with Him, tell Him all your thoughts, reveal to Him your depths, with all frankness, in all honesty, with full confidence, with an open heart, never growing tired of talking with Him.

If God exists in your life, your life will be righteousness and joy. It will be a life of love and peace. Rather, your life will be a visual image of the kingdom of God on earth. How beautiful it is to be

---

[1] The entire previous section is excerpted from *Being with God*. Throughout the book, since this is a fresh translation from the Arabic, general references are given to book titles, and not page numbers or chapters. Please note that occasionally the sentences are rearranged and/or His Holiness's words are paraphrased to give flow to the articles, addressing God or the reader.

with God. It is the delight of the spirit here on earth, and the spirit's eternal bliss in heaven.[2]

There is no eternal bliss, except God. All other bliss is not real. Full permanent pleasure is in God, it is what no eye can see, nor ear hear. This is the real kingdom: to live with God, and in God, forever, without hindrance.[3]

[2] Excerpted from *Love, the Pinnacle of All Virtues.*
[3] Excerpted from *God and Nothing Else.*

1. YOU, O LORD, ALONE[4]

*Y*ou, O Lord, are not outside me, but You are inside me. When I remember You, I go beyond simply lifting up my eyes to the highest (because You are not contained in heaven), rather, You are inside me; I do not need to search for You outside.

True was that writer who said: "I close my eyes, and yet I see You." You are above the senses; I set aside these senses temporarily, in order to find You. If my mind is occupied by the senses—seeing, hearing, touching—they distract me from You. Oh, that I would forget all, and only You remain, to satisfy my life.

Oh, that You, O Lord, were my only portion, having no other portion. Take everything I have, and give me Yourself; give me the grace of knowing You. I do not want to make many requests; I want You, only You. I want everything to lose its value in my eyes, and for You alone to remain of value to me. For only You do I care. I love You, the God who dwells in my heart, and not just the God whom I read about in books.

---

[4] Excerpted from *God and Nothing Else.*

2. O LORD, YOU SHEPHERD ME

When I knew You, O Lord, and tasted Your love, all emotions diminished before me, and all love was found to be shallow and superficial. Your love is the only one reaching deep within.[5]

Lord, what should I ask of You, when "You have not left me in need of any of the works of Your honor?"[6] You, O Lord, shepherd me, so that I shall not want. All that You have given me, even until now, is too much for me. You have given me above and beyond what I asked and above what I deserve. I feel Your abundance, short in nothing whatsoever.

Besides, Lord, I do not know what is good for me, so as to request it. You know what I need; You give me even without me asking! You have taught us: "Therefore do not worry about tomorrow, for tomorrow will worry about its own things... But seek first the kingdom of God and His righteousness, and all these things shall be added to you" (Mt 6:34, 33). I dared to remind You of what is pleasant to Your eye; do to me according to the abundance of Your fatherly tenderness. All I ask is that You forgive my sins, and introduce Your kingdom into my life.

Moreover, I, my Lord, am ashamed to ask, given all the sins I have committed! I am ashamed to ask,

---

[5] Excerpted from *God and Nothing Else*.
[6] H G Bishop Serapion, and H G Bishop Youssef. 2007. *The Divine Liturgies: The Anaphoras of Saints Basil, Gregory, and Cyril*. 2nd Edition. Dallas: Coptic Orthodox Diocese of the Southern United States, 272.

since I have disobeyed many of Your commandments and neglected my duties toward You, having no longer boldness with which to make any requests. Shame covers my face, and remembrance of my sins entangles my tongue from asking. Lord, forgive me.

But how can I ask for something new, when I have not thanked You for Your previous gifts to me? I say, "Bless the Lord, O my soul; and all that is within me, bless His holy name! Bless the Lord, O my soul, and forget not all His benefits" (Ps 103:1, 2). You, O Lord, have given me much in abundance, and I have not yet thanked You for all the generosity You have bestowed upon me. Oh, that I would live the life of thanksgiving, not of demand! I say with the psalmist in the psalm: "What shall I render to the Lord for all His benefits toward me? I will take up the cup of salvation, and call upon the name of the Lord… I will pay my vows to the Lord now in the presence of all His people" (Ps 116:12-14).[7]

---

[7] Excerpted from *Life of Humility and Meekness*.

3. WHO AM I, O LORD[8]

*W*ho am I, O Lord, what is my strength, and what is my understanding, that I can solve my problems? You, O Lord, know my problems more than I know them; You know the hidden and the apparent—the problems clear to me, the ones hidden from my eyes, and the ones to come.

Yes, You, O Lord, are the one working in me (all the while that I do not work). You are my Engine; You are my Director. You work with me, work through me, and work in me. Perhaps I cannot see You, yet I feel You, through a spiritual vision inside me, one that my tongue cannot express. I know You, but words are too weak to express this knowledge.

In Your wisdom, O Lord, You are able to solve every problem. And in Your love, You are willing. I am firmly sure that You love me more than I love myself, and You protect me more than I protect myself. I am a little one before You, and yet, "the Lord is the keeper of little ones" (Ps 114:6).[9] Therefore, I leave everything in Your hands, and rest in faith, confident that You have many solutions; I am confident that "unless the Lord builds the house, they labor in vain who build it; unless the Lord guards the city, the watchman stays awake in vain" (Ps 127:1).

---

[8] Excerpted from *God and Nothing Else*.
[9] The Douay-Rheims American Edition.

As long as You, O my Lord, see my weariness, this is enough for me. You, O Almighty, preserve justice on earth. You comfort the weary, carrying our sufferings and pains. I do not trouble myself with my problems, but leave them in Your hands "and there is none upon earth that I desire besides You" (Ps 73:25). "I am with you at all times." Lord, Oh that I would forget all, and You alone remain, satisfying my life.

4. MAY YOUR WILL BE DONE[10]

O Lord, I submit to Your will, because I love Your will from my depth, trusting in You and in it. This, Your will, has repaired my thoughts and repaired my judgments on issues. It has corrected my path and my way. How beautiful are Your ways, O Lord: "How unsearchable are His judgments and His ways past finding out!" (Rom 11:33). This, Your will, is the most beautiful song in my mouth, and the sweetest news to my ears. Therefore, let Your will be done.

There is no better will for me than Yours. Next to it, I feel the ignorance of any will that contradicts it, whether for myself or for another person. It is sufficient for us, O Lord, for Your cloud to be over our heads, and the pillar of fire in front of us (Ex 13:21). We do not determine our course, but rather, Your goodwill determines it.

As for us, we rejoice to be under Your leadership. Wherever Your cloud leads, we will follow, and wherever it stops, we will take shelter under its shade (Ex 40:36-38). We delight to see the fog above the Ark of the Covenant which represents Your presence. Let the tabernacle move in the wilderness into the unknown. It is unknown to us, but it is in Your knowledge and understanding since eternity. This is enough, for us to take our steps into this unknown, in full assurance that we are on the road to Canaan. Your

---

[10] Excerpted from *Life of Faith.*

judgments, O Lord, are above my knowledge, and Your works are above my understanding. Who am I before You? All my knowledge is foolishness in front of You.

I take from You by submitting, not by analyzing.

Give me, O Lord, the faith of a babe, and not the faith of philosophers and wise men, because "You have hidden these things from the wise and prudent and revealed them to babes" (Lk 10:21).

Blessed are You, O Lord, who created this human mind, bestowed on it all these abilities, and revealed to it Your creation in the forces of nature. If Your earthly servants know all this, how much more do You, the unlimited Almighty? Thus, our faith is strengthened by attributing all power and all wonders to You, O God.

Give me, O Lord, to believe You with perfect faith. Give me to love You and trust You in everything, and to believe that You use me for good, no matter how dark the world seems before me. Help me feel that my mind is much smaller than to understand Your wisdom and judgments. I know that You are gracious, that You are loving, that You see everything, and that You are almighty. And yet, often I weaken; strengthen my feeble faith.

5. I WANT TO LIVE WITH YOU[11]

O Lord, in case I am not serious about saving my soul, You, O Lord, are serious about saving this soul. If this is a salvation that my will is unable to bring about, no doubt Your grace enables and strengthens it. If I do not want life with You, it is enough that You want for me to live with You, and Your will does the rest. Lord, if You leave me to my will and my weakness, I will be lost. Consider me a patient, unable to heal myself, unable even to go to the doctor. Say a word and my soul shall live. I will not leave You, until I feel that You have accepted me, and returned me to You and to Your love.

I not only want You to forgive me my sin, but I want You to absolutely remove from my heart all love for sin... I come to You as I am, with my sin, and it is You who takes it away from me. If I were able to leave the love of sin, I would have returned to You long ago. Please save me from sin, to lead me in Your triumphal procession (Cf. 2 Cor 2:14). Remove the love of sin from my heart, and remove its control over my will. Amen.

---

[11] Excerpted from *Return to God*.

6. RETURN US, O LORD, THAT WE MAY RETURN TO YOU[12]

O Lord, I seek Your will, but I do not know the steps to find it. Therefore, each day I say with the psalmist in the psalms: "Cause me to know the way in which I should walk. Teach me to do Your will. Your Spirit leads me in uprightness" (Cf. Ps 143:8-10). I also say, "Guide me in Your way so that I walk in Your truth. Show me, O Lord, Your paths. Guide me in an upright way." Teach me the steps.

The Psalmist also says in the great Psalm: "I am a stranger in the earth; do not hide Your commandments from me... Blessed are You, O Lord! Teach me Your statutes! [Blessed are You, O Lord,] revive me in Your righteousness... Teach me to do Your will" (Ps 119:19, 12, 40; 143:10). We say in the Divine Liturgy, "Lead us throughout the way into Your kingdom."[13] We say in the conclusion to each prayer, "Ease our life and guide us to fulfill Your commandments."[14] I, O Lord, often fall and stray away from You, but You say, "Return to Me... and I will return to you" (Zech 1:3). I want to discuss this matter with You. How can we return to You, if *You* do not return to us? Return to us, so as to return us to You.

---

[12] Excerpted from *Dialogue with God*.
[13] (H and H 2007), 219.
[14] Azmy, Fr. Abraham, ed. 2009. *The Agpeya: The Coptic Prayer Book of the Seven Hours.* Hamden: Virgin Mary and Archangel Michael Coptic Orthodox Church, 34.

Which comes first? Do we return to You, or do You return to us, in order to return us to You?

In the story of the lost sheep, it was impossible for the lost sheep to return to You; You are the one who went and searched for it, found it, and carried it on Your shoulder, rejoicing (Lk 15:5). Likewise, the lost coin (Lk 15:8-10), it was unable to return to its purse, but You searched for it, and returned it to You.

Adam, who fled from You, and hid behind the trees (Gen 3:8-9), did You tell him, "Return to Me and I will return to You?" He was unable to return to You. You are the one who returned to him; You are the one who searched for him and returned him to You. Jonah, who fled from You, You are the one who returned him. Elijah, who fled in the wilderness saying, "The children of Israel have forsaken Your covenant, torn down Your altars, and killed Your prophets with the sword. I alone am left" (1 Kg 19:10), You are the one who returned him to You. Thomas, who doubted You and said I will not believe in the resurrection except if I put my finger in the place of the nails (Jn 20:24-25), You are the one who appeared to him.

The disciples who feared and hid (Jn 20:19), You are the one who returned to them in order to return them to You. Saul of Tarsus, who persecuted the church, daily dragging men and women to the prisons (Acts 8:3), he was not the one who returned to You, but You are the one who returned to him, in order to return him to You. All this, and yet You say, "Return to Me... and I will return to you" (Zech 1:3). No Lord, on our own, we do not know how to return; alone we are unable to return, as You personally said in John 15:5: "Without Me you can do nothing." Therefore, we are unable to return to You without You; You are the one who returns us to You.

You also said in the Psalms: "Unless the Lord builds the house, they labor in vain who build it; unless the Lord guards the city, the watchman stays awake in vain" (Ps 127:1).

How can we build our spiritual lives without You? How can we protect ourselves from diabolic attacks without Your protection? The starting point is from You. You say, "You must ask," and yet, Your grace is what makes us ask. The responsibility for our repentance: is it our responsibility or Your responsibility? Do we repent, or do we say, as said in Jeremiah: "Restore me, and I will return, for You are the Lord my God" (Jer 31:18). I want to repent, but it is You who brings me to repentance; without You I cannot repent. Bring me to repentance, O Lord, so that I may repent. Return me, O Lord, that I may return. Return us, O Lord, God of our salvation. "Bring back our captivity, O Lord, as the streams in the South... Restore us, O Lord God of hosts; cause Your face to shine, and we shall be saved!" (Ps 126:4; 80:19). You, O Lord say: "Return to Me... and I will return to you" (Zech 1:3). We want to return to You, so that You return us to You—this is Your divine work. You are the Good Shepherd. You shepherd us in green pastures, You lead us beside still waters, You restore our souls and lead us to the paths of righteousness. Even if we walk in the valley of the shadow of death, we will not fear evil for You are with us (Ps 23).

You say, O Lord, in the Book of Ezekiel the prophet, "'I will feed My flock, and I will make them lie down,' says the Lord God. 'I will seek what was lost and bring back what was driven away, bind up the broken and strengthen what was sick'" (Ezek 34:15-16). Do You think that the lost can return by himself, if You do not seek him? You say I seek the lost; seek him then, and pursue him, and bring back the driven away; because the one driven away cannot return himself. You are the one who binds the broken and strengthens the sick. One of Your children comes to You, O Lord, saying, "Give me my share of the inheritance," takes his share, and leaves. Will You let him go far away? Behold, he has gone, and tasted toil, and returned again. Yet, there are many people who have walked out of Your house, were lost, and did not return. They are the majority! You say, "Therefore I will save My flock, and they shall no longer be a prey" (Ezek 34:22). Do You think that Your sheep are able to save themselves, if You do not save them? You say, "I will make a covenant of peace with them, and cause wild beasts to cease from the land… I will deliver My flock from their mouths, that they may no longer be food for them" (Ezek 34:25, 10).

So, where are these promises of Yours, O Lord? Where are Your promises? Where are Your promises in which You said, "'I am with you always, even to the end of the age.' Amen" (Mt 28:20)? Where are Your promises in which You said, "The gates of Hades shall not prevail against it" (Mt 16:18)? Where are Your promises in which You said to the church, "See, I have inscribed you on the palms of My hands" (Is 49:16)? Also, where You said that even if a mother forgets her newborn, yet I will not forget you: "Can a woman forget her nursing child, and not have compassion on the son of her womb? Surely they may forget, yet I will not forget you" (Is 49:15).

"My sheep hear My voice, and I know them, and they follow Me. And I give them eternal life, and they shall never perish; neither shall anyone snatch them out of My hand" (Jn 10:27-28). Oh, Lord, the snatchers are plenty! Where is Your clutching hand, from which were snatched many of Your children? Where is Your kingdom on earth? Look at the map, where do You see Your kingdom? You say: "Narrow is the gate and difficult is the way which leads to life, and there are few who find it" (Mt 7:14). Why, Lord, do only a few find it? Why are only a few saved? You are the one "who desires all men to be saved and to come to the knowledge of the truth" (1 Tim 2:4). It is You who said to the Father "I have kept them in Your truth so that none of them perished" (Cf. Jn 17:12). We address You, Lord, because You are a compassionate God, not seeking the death of the sinner, but that he should return and live. We address You because You are a powerful God who is able to save. Have You saved all? We address You because You are a mighty God. We address You because You are a humble God who accepts dialogue with us. We address You because You are a wise God who can bring sweetness out of barrenness; yet the barren remain barren! Behold, deviations fill the whole earth: religious deviations, behavioral deviations, intellectual deviations, while You, O Lord, see and consider the earth full of corruption. What remains is for You to work.

Where is Your care and where is Your protection? I know that You care and protect; therefore, David tells You: "Show us Your strength, O Lord, and show us Your salvation" (Cf. Ps 85:7).

Why should they say, "Where is your God" (Ps 42:10)? Where, O Lord, is the work of Your grace, and where is the work of Your Holy Spirit?

1 Corinthians 12: 3 says, "No one can say that Jesus is Lord except by the Holy Spirit" (1 Cor 12:3). Where, O Lord, is Your salvation, when You have come to save that which was lost: "For the Son of Man has come to save that which was lost" (Mt 18:11)?

You also said: I did not come to judge the world but to save the world" (Jn 12:47). Where is Your work in the world now? Where is Your fiery Spirit? Where are the gifts of Your Holy Spirit, as He worked in olden days? As You said: "I will pour out My Spirit on all flesh... I will show wonders in heaven above and signs in the earth beneath" (Acts 2:17, 19).

I know the problem: the free will You gave us (humans abused free will against themselves), and also the principle of equal opportunity which You gave to the devil. The devil exploited it for the destruction of the world. Is there no limit to free will on earth! Do You leave people to their own free will, to their own destruction? You see a person throw himself into the sea and drown and would You say, "Leave him to his own free will"? When one commits suicide, will You say, "Leave him to his free will"? People destroy themselves through their free will; will You leave them to their own free will?

Oh that You, Lord, would interfere in this free will, and control people's free will; I know You would answer, "I do not want to force them to do good." Truly, You do not want to force us, but please help us to do good. Guide us! Aid us! You say, "Assuredly, I say to you, unless you are converted and become as little children, you will by no means enter the kingdom of heaven" (Mt 18:3). So be it. Treat us as children then; the child needs one to carry him and one who bears with him.

7. LEAVE ME ALONE![15]

(This meditation is not for everyone. It speaks to a certain spiritual level. Those who have not attained it will gain no benefit.)

*B*ehold, O Lord, I am constantly interfering with what does not concern me... When will the time come when I will not interfere in my own affairs, but rather leave them to You—wherever You lead me, I walk, however You form me, I become. When will I be satisfied with the condition that You select for me, so that I do not nag You to change it, as if You are unaware of what is good for me? When will my prayer turn from requests to thanks? When will I set out searching, only to find nothing, because I cannot find anything better for me than my current condition?

When will I believe in You in full faith, and so entrust You with my life to manage as You see fit, You who only do good. I wish I didn't have to force myself into Your work; I wish I didn't spy and snoop on You to see what You are doing with me! How You are working! Is Your work acceptable (to me) or not? Do I need to interfere, or not? Oh Lord, when will You liberate me from my *self*? When? Not so that I become a saint, but so that I may find You.

My *self* is not mine, but is Yours. You have purchased it with Your precious blood, You own it. I no longer have any right to interfere in its affairs,

---

[15] Excerpted from *Release of the Spirit*.

because You manage them according to Your good will. I am to watch and glorify You. When will the time come, when my only job will be but to leave my *self* between Your hands, and forget it there, remembering only those two hands which formed and fashioned me, the hands You placed on each person to heal.

When will my faith in You be complete so that I may entrust You with my life to do as You please, without forcing myself into this work of Yours, O Creator of all goodness? Oh Lord, how ignorantly I behave towards You! I interfere in Your wise work, trying to halt it, in order to enforce my own counsel! How much wiser it would be for me to just keep silent, observing rather than participating. Then I shall see the wonders of Your wisdom.

O Lord, I often think of myself, but I do not think of You, not even a little. I trust much in myself, but I do not trust in You, not even a little. My *self* is my idol. When will it be crushed, so that I can worship You in truth? I must break this idol, and because it is beautiful in my eyes, or because it is dearly beloved to me, O Lord, step in and crush it. Then You will have no rival in my heart, I will love only You; You will have no competitor in my faith, and I will adore You. O Lord, if I thought of You as much as I think of myself, if I count on You as much as I rely on my own ability, if I love You as much as I love myself, I would have become as those saints who denied themselves that they may know You.

When will You liberate my soul from imprisonment, and release Your servant in peace? When will I lose my *self* for Your sake to find You? Then I will find my *self* in You. When will I destroy my *self* for Your sake, so that it lives in You? When will I seek my *self*, to not find it, but to find You; when will I look at it and see You? When will I look at the world or people, only to find You in them? May You become everything to me, with nothing besides You.

People told me: "Know yourself." They also told me: "Enter into yourself." Oh Lord, this *self* of mine is the cause of all my troubles. When will I enter into it, to not find it?

How many times did I look at my *self* and find it hanging on the cross motionless. When I looked closely, I found You, so I rejoiced. I did not rejoice in my *self* because it inherited the kingdom, but I rejoiced in You, in that I found You. I imagine that I will not find You each time, except there in the valley of the shadow of death, because if I walk through the valley of the shadow of death, there You are with me. You created us for life, but through our sins we chose death. You who are simple, to whom all things are pure, You sanctify death and make it a door of life for us! It is the only door of life. "He who finds his life [his soul] will lose it, and he who loses his life for My sake

18

will find it" (Mt 10:39). Deny yourself, take up your cross, and follow Me (Mt 16:24).

In the first year of my monastic life, I read writings of the saints saying that monasticism is to detach from all to attach to the One. To the best of my ability, I locked myself off from the world and from people, but this did not bring me to attach to You, because I did not enter solitude for Your sake, but for myself, to accept myself, or for people to approve of me.

But, in the second year, total detachment had a different meaning for me; it meant detachment from my *self*, because I had previously established it as supreme in my life.

In the third year, what will this phrase mean to me? I do not know. Oh, that I would forget it, and forget pondering its meaning, being exceedingly preoccupied with You.

I used to tell my brethren that our gathering together here on earth delays our preoccupation with God, and perhaps this will hinder our coming together there with Him in eternity. Now I want to say that my *gathering* with my *self* is what hinders me even more.

I feel a need, whenever I retreat into myself, to tell it to "leave me now." This is better for us. Leave me so that I may retreat with God, and so I will be able to enjoy His promises, that you "shall be established before Me" (Jer 30:20).

I sit, not with my *self*, but with God who dwells in me.

8. You, and You Alone, O Lord[16]

O Lord, I cannot find any other being except You who understands me, who assures me, to whom I can open up my heart, tell all my secrets, and explain all my weaknesses, which You hear without despising. I pour my tears out before You, and confide in You my longings. With You I do not feel alone, but with me is a Heart that embraces me, and Strength that supports me. Without You, O Lord, I feel like I am in a vacuum; I do not see a true existence to myself. You are Emmanuel—God with us. My soul longs for Your whole Spirit. It longs for what is more excellent than the material, the world, and everything in it. Yes, within my soul there is a longing for the Unlimited, insatiable by any other.

I do not deserve anything, but, despite all my sins, Your patience encourages me, and Your compassionate heart consoles me. You are the gentle God who does not wish the death of a sinner but that he should return and live (Cf. Ezek 32:18). In me, the stillborn (1 Cor 15:8), the might of Your mercy is unveiled.

---

[16] Excerpted from *Spiritual Means.*

9. I WANT YOU, O LORD[17]

O Lord, I want You. I want to go back to You. Snatch me from where I am, and draw me to You once more. As You, O Lord, gave me the commandments, give me the power to fulfill them.

Without You I am nothing. I lost my life when I lost You. I lost my delight and my happiness, and my life became tasteless. I, O Lord, I want to go back to You, but, my enemies have prevailed against me... they rejoice if I am moved (Cf. Ps 13:4). "Many are they who say of me, 'There is no help for him in God'" (Ps 3:2).

I lost my strength when I stayed away from You, so please give me of Your own strength. Give me divine aid, with which to return to You. I sit before You, O Lord; I will not rise from here except after taking from You a special blessing, and feel that You have returned me to You and consider me one of Your children.

I not only want You to forgive my sin, but I want You to completely remove all love for sin from my heart. I cannot return to You as long as the love for sin remains in my heart. What should I do? Do I wait until the love for sin fades from my heart, and then return to You? Yet, I cannot be rid of it without You!

Behold, I come to You as I am, bearing my sins, and You are the one who strips them from me. If I

---

[17] Excerpted from *Return to God.*

were able to leave the love of sin, I would have returned to You long ago. Rescue me from them, to lead me in Your triumphal procession (Cf. 2 Cor 2:14). Strip their love from my heart, and strip their control over my will, "Purge me with hyssop, and I shall be clean; wash me, and I shall be whiter than snow" (Ps 51:7).

As You have given me, O Lord, the commandments, give me power to fulfill them.

I will not leave You until I feel that You have accepted me to You, and returned me to You and to Your love.

Do the weak fail to reach Your kingdom, O Lord? Behold, I am weak, unable by my human arms to reach, so grasp my hand, and do not leave me to my weakness. Wash and cleanse me, as You have washed and cleansed others. Have You not said, "Ask, and it will be given to you"? (Mt 7:7). Behold, I ask! Have You not said, "Whatever you ask the Father in My name He will give you" (Jn 16:23)? Behold, I ask. I will hang onto all Your promises, demanding them. At least, I will hang onto this promise: "I will give you a new heart and put a new spirit within you; I will take the heart of stone out of your flesh and give you a heart of flesh. I will put My Spirit within you and cause you to walk in My statutes, and you will keep My judgments and do them" (Ezek 36:26-27).

Where are these promises in me, O Lord? Behold, I stand here, clinging onto the horns of the altar.

Those who pray for two minutes and leave, I am unlike them; I will remain here for You, O Lord. I will not end my prayer until it concludes with You having graced me with repentance and returned me to You. Forgive my boldness, O Lord; I am Your young child. And if I am mistaken, treat me as a young son who knows nothing. The Holy Bible says: "If you then, being evil, know how to give good gifts to your children, how much more will your Father who is in heaven give good things to those who ask Him" (Mt 7:11). You, as a compassionate Father, know how to give good gifts to Your children.

10. GRANT THE SPIRIT FROM YOUR RESOURCES[18]

O Lord, forgive me if I pray without fervor; I'm praying from the emptiness in my heart. You give me the fervor. It is You who pours out Your Holy Fire into my heart. Take my prayers as is, with their shortcomings. Things do not start out perfect; perfection is from You. I pray, even if without spirit, and You grant me the Spirit. My Lord, will I sin and say that by my human arm and my crumbling will, that I will turn into a spiritual person? No, but by Your might, Your blessing, Your grace, and Your Holy Spirit I will become the image You want for me.

Guide me... hold my hand and lead me step by step, as You would lead a young child learning to walk: "Restore us, O God of our salvation" (Ps 85:4). "Bring back our captivity, O Lord, as the streams in the South... Then our mouth was filled with laughter, and our tongue with singing... The Lord has done great things for us, and we are glad" (Ps 126:4, 2, 3).

---

[18] Excerpted from *Return to God.*

11. Out of the Depth of my Heart I Cried to You[19]

*F*rom the depth of my heart, from the depth of my thoughts, from the depth of my feelings and emotions, I cried to You. I cried to You from the depth of my need for You. From the depth of my weakness and weariness, from the depth of my downfall, I need Your forgiveness. Out of the depth of misery brought about by my sin, I cried to you. It is from the depth of my feelings of helplessness and failure, which drag me down to fear. "Out of the depths I have cried to You, O Lord; Lord, hear my voice!" (Ps 130:1-2).

Out of the depth of the problems that surround me, unresolved except by You; from the depth of the troubles and trials, which come from people and from the devil; from the depth of the dangers I feel closing in on me; out of the depth of my self-shame, seeing my weaknesses and mistakes; out of the depth of the abyss in which I am, like Jonah, who fleeing from You prayed, "I cried out to the Lord because of my affliction, and He answered me. Out of the belly of Sheol I cried, and You heard my voice" (Jon 2:2); out of the depth of my sorrow over myself; out of the depth of my fear; out of all these depths I cried to You, O Lord, so please hear my voice.

As for me, from the depths, I cry to You out of the depths. I cry to You, so that You raise me out of it.

---

[19] Excerpted from *Meditations on the Psalms and Litanies of Compline.*

You are He who "raises the poor out of the dust, and lifts the needy out of the ash heap" (Ps 113:7). I, out of the depth of my weakness, cried out to the depth of Your power; from the depth of my need, I cried out to the depth of Your tenderness and love; from the depth of my fall, I cried out to the depth of Your forgiveness; from the depth of my problems, from the depth of the abyss, I cried up to the height of Your heaven.

I cried out to the depth of Your wisdom, which solves all problems.

12. LET MY PRAYER COME BEFORE YOU[20]

*B*ehold, O Lord, I cry out to You from the depth of my heart. I bellow out to You as a child calling tearfully to his father, his aid. Likewise, I cry out to You, O compassionate one, O Omnipotent. It is a cry for help, a cry of faith, of hope, and of need—an adamant cry. This reminds me of the Egyptian poet, who in one of his poems explained the force of this cry: "My voice is like the cry of one sinking, hollering out to a lifeboat. He cries, cries, cries, he cries out all he can—for his life." It is a scream, not just a cry. A cry that attracts Your gentleness, O Lord.

I cry out to You, O Lord, for You to hear my prayer, for my prayer to come before You, for You to accept it, despite my sins and unworthiness, although I sense the familiarity between us is absent. All I want is for my prayer to reach You; I leave the rest to Your love—You who do not treat me according to my sins, but according to Your mercy. We know that requests reach You, even if we do not pray, as You preceded and said, "I have surely seen the oppression of My people who are in Egypt, and have heard their cry because of their taskmasters, for I know their sorrows. So I have come down to deliver them" (Ex 3:7-8). All this and they had not prayed yet!

"Lord, hear my voice!" (Ps 130:2). Help me feel that You have received my prayer, took note of it, and that

---

[20] Excerpted from *Meditations on the Psalms and Litanies of Compline.*

my cry has reached Your ear; this is sufficient for me. I pray, for You to hear my prayers; I will persist in prayer until I am certain. I am confident once You hear my prayer, You will act. For Your name's sake, I await Your salvation. I wait until I receive Your aid, and until I earn Your forgiveness. What is this name on which I waited? Your name: the Savior. Of You, the angel of annunciation said: "And she will bring forth a Son, and you shall call His name Jesus, for He will save His people from their sins" (Mt 1:21). The word Jesus means Savior.

I have also waited for Your name: "'Immanuel,' which is translated, 'God with us'" (Mt 1:23). As long as You are with us, I will wait for Your work *in* us, and Your work *for* us.

I wait for Your gentle compassionate forgiving name, who "has not dealt with us according to our sins, nor punished us according to our iniquities" (Ps 103:10). You are described: "The Lord is merciful and gracious, slow to anger, and abounding in mercy. He will not always strive with us, nor will He keep His anger forever" (Ps 103:8-9). For this name, I waited, full of hope. I waited, confident that You will work in me for repentance and forgiveness. You will work in me to fulfill Your commandments and laws.

My soul waits for Your law. It waits until I am able to fulfill Your law, it waits for Your aid which will enable me to fulfill all Your words "more than those who watch for the morning" (Ps 130:6). Those in the dark eagerly watch the coming of the morning. Behold, I watch the coming of Your morning; when it will come to dispel my darkness.

13. I Confess Before You, O Lord[21]

O Lord, I confess before You that my direction in words needs to change. I shamefully confess before You that I have often spoken to people about virtue, and rarely have I spoken to them about You, while You should be all in all.

In order for me to speak about You, I need to know You. How can I know You, being a limited human being? How can I know You who are unlimited, incomprehensible, the unapproachable light, the One whom man cannot see and live?

I tried to ask Your saints, who knew You, or about You with a partial knowledge, so I approached St. Paul the Apostle, who ascended to the third heaven, and I asked him about You. He said that he heard and saw things "which it is not lawful for a man to utter" (2 Cor 12:4). Likewise, John the Beloved, who saw an open door in heaven, and glimpsed the throne of God, did not explain to us his vision except in symbols that cannot give a complete picture.

Sometimes I ask myself: "Is it arrogance of me to try to know You, while I remain ignorant of my own self, and ignorant of many human and material issues?" If I do not know the essence of my soul, how could I know the Creator of this soul? If I still do not know Your heaven and angels, how can I know Your divine essence?

---

[21] Excerpted from *Release of the Spirit*.

All I know about You is what You freely reveal to us. You do not reveal to us, except what our souls can handle, because, if You reveal to us more, our human nature will halt in awe of fascination, our minds will stop understanding, our linguistic vocabulary will fail to express, and we will confess that what we are seeing cannot be uttered.

I try, in knowing You, to come out from the scope of books, with all their depth, sometimes even coming beyond the limits of mental knowledge, to give my spirit its vast space to launch out and excel in capabilities, talents, and knowledge. It suffers greatly from the haze of this physical body.

We wonder, O Lord, will we know You in Your eternal kingdom? Will we see You then face to face, as Your servant St. Paul claimed? I find myself truly baffled by this phrase: "Face to face" (1 Cor 3:12).

In the kingdom, despite the glorified resurrection, and the luminous spiritual bodies we will have, surely, we will remain—as we are—limited human beings. You will reveal to us a little something about Yourself that we did not know in the world; we will rejoice and be elated with this. Then You will gradually reveal to us a little more and more, as much as we can handle.

Perhaps You will reveal to us more, and each soul will cry out, lovesick, "Enough! Enough!" (Prov 30:16). You will continue to expand our hearts, expand our souls, to be able to understand You even more. You remain unlimited. We continue, as we are, limited. Despite our expansion, we remain limited, gaining only little knowledge of You.

Time passes in eternity, while we enjoy knowing You, we "taste and see that the Lord is good" (Ps 34:8), continually discovering something new about You, feeding on this sweet satiating knowledge, yet we cannot know You altogether.

When then will we truly know You? Our Lord Jesus answers: "And this is eternal life, that they may know You, the only true God, and Jesus Christ whom you have sent" (Jn 17:3). Therefore, knowing You is not a subject of years or days, but its path is the entirety of eternity, endless eternity. If this is so in eternity, what then can we say about our ignorance on earth? Do we really know anything?

Therefore, I beg You, O great Creator, to pardon me if I speak to people about virtues more than I speak to them of You.

This is for two reasons. The first reason is that I do not know You. This I know, that I pray You to reveal to me something about Yourself, and what You reveal to me, that I will inform people, so that they may experience a taste of the kingdom on earth. The second reason is that when I speak to them about virtues, I want them to prepare their hearts to know You. I want them to raise Vespers and Matins incense on this heart, until it deserves to have the divine mysteries offered on it.

We, of ourselves, do not know You. However, we want, through Your grace, to prepare ourselves to know You. This knowledge comes from You, in what You reveal to us, and not through our mental effort, not even through our spiritual effort. All our mental and spiritual efforts—though necessary—in truth fall under the meaning of prayer or begging, for the cloud to fill the house, for the fire to ignite in the bush, until the Lord reveals Himself. Then, the heart falls prostrate in reverence, and sings with thanksgiving, "[You] have given to me the learning of Your knowledge."[22]

This divine knowledge is the pearl of great price, which the merchant sold all that he had and bought it (Cf. Mt 13: 45-46). Perhaps, among the possessions he sold was vast human intelligence, which we hoard in our minds, and which occupies all our time so that we are not free to know You. It prevents us from sitting with Mary at Your feet pouring into our hearts that living water, which quenches the thirst, never to thirst again.

If only we would seek after intelligence, asking for it with all our hearts, finding it within, deep within our depth, where You live, where Your holy temple abides, which was consecrated by You on the day of holy baptism.

---

[22] (H and H 2007), 272.

14. COME LORD AND REIGN, BEHOLD I AM YOURS[23]

O Lord, if Your kingdom is not of this world, come, I have a kingdom suitable for You to lay Your head and rest. You might find Your rest in my heart. If You find in it disobedience or rebelliousness, then, "gird Your sword upon Your thigh, O Mighty One, with Your glory and Your majesty" (Ps 45:3).

Come, O Lord, reign; let Your kingdom come in my heart, and in the hearts of all people. Let Your kingdom come on all nations and in all countries, "that Your way may be known on earth, your salvation among all nations" (Ps 67:2). O Lord, push away from me anything that hinders Your kingdom within me. Push away from me the ego that prevented the Jewish chief priests from Your kingdom. Push away from me the literalism that kept the Pharisees from Your kingdom. Push away from me jealousy and envy which kept away the scribes, elders, and leaders. Come, O Lord, in strength, and purify my altar also; "Do you not know that you are the temple of God and that the Spirit of God dwells in you?" (1 Cor 3:16). Come, Lord, and cleanse my sanctuary. Overturn the tables therein, before they overturn me and fritter away my eternity. Do not abandon my heart to its wishes, desires, and emotions, until it becomes as a market used for selling and buying, but, "purge me

---

[23] Excerpted from *Meditations on Great Friday*.

with [Your] hyssop, and I shall be clean" (Ps 51:7), then I can sing with You, "My house shall be called a house of prayer" (Mt 21:13). Lord, please do this quickly before Your sanctuary is destroyed!

O, You who entered Your temple, cleansed it with Your zealous love, and sat teaching in it, oh that You would enter into my depth and cleanse my heart. By Your authority, overturn greed for money and the world, evict carnal desires, and prevent any thoughts that do not please Your goodness from passing through. You alone have this authority. I beg You to enter the sanctuary of my heart today; I will rejoice once You reign in me, and illuminate its darkness with Your life-giving teachings; this day will become a sacred feast to me. Give me, my Lord Jesus Christ, the good harp of David the Prophet, "The sound of harpists playing their harps" (Rev 14:2), to chant the praise of children, and cheer with them today: "Hosanna in the highest… Blessed is He who comes in the name of the Lord" (Mt 21:9).

15. LORD, TEACH ME HUMILITY[24]

Teach me, O Lord, humility and lowliness, as You advised from Your blessed mouth: "Learn from Me, for I am gentle and lowly in heart" (Mt 11:29). I meditate on Your ascent to Jerusalem. It was humble, which is not strange for You; humility is in all Your actions.

Permit me, O Lord, to hear that voice so beloved to my soul, Your words: "Fear not, daughter of Zion" (Jn 12:15). Oh, that I would rise today and spread the road before You with those who spread garments on the road, with those who "washed their robes and made them white in the blood of the Lamb" (Rev 7:14), so that I may learn how to decorate the road before You with acts of love and the rest of the virtues.

Oh, that I were the gate of the temple, that royal door by which You entered into Jerusalem, the holy city: "Each individual gate was of one pearl. And the street of the city was pure gold, like transparent glass" (Rev 21:21). Oh, that I were counted, this day, among those precious rational stones in Your holy temple, "The foundations of the wall of the city were adorned with all kinds of precious stones" (Rev 21:19).

Arise my soul, ascend to your Savior, to heavenly Jerusalem, "And behold, a great multitude which no one could number, of all nations, tribes, peoples, and tongues, standing before the throne and before the

---

[24] Excerpted from *Meditations on Great Friday*.

Lamb, clothed with white robes, with palm branches in their hands, and crying out with a loud voice, saying, 'Salvation belongs to our God who sits on the throne, and to the Lamb!'" (Rev 7:9-10).

16. SAVE ME, O LORD[25]

*S*ave me, O Lord, from my heart, from my sins, and from my nature, so that they do not hinder peace with You. You changed the hearts of many who were perhaps stages worse off than me. Oh, I pray that I would be one of them! You, O Lord, changed the heart of St. Moses the Strong, St. Augustine, St. Mary the Copt (the Egyptian), and Arianus the governor of Antinoe. Would my case be difficult for You? Consider me a complicated case, yet, it is not difficult against Your infinite ability. I, O Lord, am unable to fix my heart in order to be reconciled with You, but it is You who fixes my heart, and places in it holy sensations befitting this reconciliation.

Did You not say, "My son, give me your heart, and let your eyes observe my ways" (Prov 23:26)? Take it as is. "Purge me with hyssop, and I shall be clean; wash me, and I shall be whiter than snow" (Ps 51:7). I do not ask You to renovate this heart, but to "create in me a clean heart, O God" (Ps 51:10). Give me a new spirit as You promised: "I will give you a new heart and put a new spirit within you" (Ezek 36:26). If there is no love for You in my heart, then give me this love. Do not blame me for my lack of love, but pour in me this love by the Holy Spirit, as Your Apostle said: "The love of God has been poured out in our hearts by the Holy Spirit who was given to us" (Rom 5:5).

---

[25] Excerpted from *Return to God.*

Consider me a young child who wants but does not know how, a child who wants but is unable, and "direct my steps" (Ps 119:133). Too often I fall.

O Lord, I want to feel Your presence; I want for You to reveal Yourself to me. I want to retreat with You, speak with You, and open up my heart to You. I want to love You more than anyone else, and more than anything, "I also count all things loss for the excellence of the knowledge of Christ Jesus my Lord, for whom I have suffered the loss of all things, and count them as rubbish, that I may gain Christ" (Phil 3:8).

17. DRAW ME AWAY! WE WILL RUN AFTER YOU[26]

*D*raw me after You, so together we will run (Cf. Song 1:4). Draw me and I will run, and all the rest of humanity will run with me. I will not walk behind You, but will run, with all my strength, as Your Apostle Paul said: "Run in such a way that you may obtain" (1 Cor 9:24). I will not run alone, but will bring with me 30, 60, and 100 others—they are the fruit of my love for You. But, what is important, O Lord, is that You draw me after You—You, rather than being pulled down by this earth from which I was taken. I was taken from earth, and perhaps to earth I will return. So, draw me to Your love and to Your service.

Tell me "follow Me" (Mt 19:4), as You told our fathers Peter and Andrew. No doubt Your word will have an amazing force that my heart will not be able to resist. When You told Matthew the tax collector, "Follow me" (Mt 9:9), that was not merely an order and an invitation, but an amazing magnetic force which detached him from the tax office. He rose up and ran after You, as did all the disciples, "for the word of God is living and powerful, and sharper than any two-edged sword" (Heb 4:12). It was able to sever all the chains binding him to the world; he found himself

---

[26] Excerpted from *Meditations on the Song of Songs.*

leaving everything, even his responsibilities at the tax office.

Draw me after You, O Lord, by Your grace, by Your Holy Spirit, by Your might, by Your angels, by all the spiritual means You have. I will run as did Augustine who converted from being an atheist to become a saintly bishop, as did many female sinners who converted instantly, not to become penitents only, but to become saints.

When the Lord Christ drew the twelve apostles to Himself, they ran after Him, and on the first day they brought with them 3,000 followers: "That day about three thousand souls were added to them" (Acts 2:41). After the miracle of healing the crippled person, those became 5,000 souls saved: "Many of those who heard the word believed; and the number of the men came to be about five thousand" (Acts 4:4). Then, multitudes of men and women were added to the Lord (Cf. Acts 5:14), and then whole towns and cities joined the faith as their spirits all ran in union with You.

18. O LORD, I LOVE YOU FROM MY DEPTH[27]

O Lord, I love You from the depth of my heart. It is true that my works are not befitting of my love for You, and yet, I do love You. My love for You is like a living seed, containing the elements of life, but its life is latent, yet unrevealed. Perhaps if given fertile soil, water, irrigation, and all the conditions for germination, this life would manifest in roots, a stem, branches, leaves, flowers, and fruits. I am so. Though the life of love is not manifest in me, that does not negate its existence.

I am not waiting until I am purified to seek You. Rather, I seek You to purify me. I will not wait until I become diligent and strong in spirit and then seek You. Rather, while I am lazy now I will seek You, to rescue me from my laziness and strengthen me. Should I repent first and then seek You? Or do I seek You saying: "Restore me, and I will return" (Jer 31:18)? Yes, I will call You while afar off so that You may draw me close.

I will seek You while on my bed, so You may awaken me. I will call out to You while sinning for You to save me. I am willing, but I have not yet walked down the road. I seek Your grace to lead me. The prodigal son did not wear the best robe while in the country feeding the swine. His father was the one

---

[27] Excerpted from *Meditations on the Song of Songs.*

who dressed him, saying, "Bring out the best robe and put it on him, and put a ring on his hand and sandals on his feet" (Lk 15:22). This was after the son returned to his father in filthy rags. O Lord, when I cried out to You, I did not call You with a mind focused on You, but while "worried and troubled about many things. But one thing is needed" (Lk 10:41, 42). Therefore, I did not find You! Perhaps I did not find You because there are barriers between You and me. Therefore, I call, but You do not answer. I shiver at Your words confronting me: "When you spread out your hands, I will hide My eyes from you; even though you make many prayers, I will not hear. Your hands are full of blood" (Is 1:15).

There are barriers between us because I have left my first love (Rev 2:4), lost the familiarity that linked me to You, and thus betrayed Your fellowship. In humiliation I feel that my words do not reach You, as if I were not Your son! I want to be reconciled with You and return to the old love that existed between us. I want to apologize to You and comfort Your heart concerning me. Yes, this is what I want.

Truly, O Lord, I am in a stage of abandonment, but I will strive behind You with full force in hopes of restoring my relationship with You. I will search for You and ask people about You until I find You.

If You abandon me, You suffer no loss, but I lose everything. If You abandon me, I will be lost, because in You is my existence, my life, and my destiny. If You abandon me, I will run after You in the streets and squares: "'I will rise now,' I said, 'And go about the city; in the streets and in the squares I will seek the one I love'" (Song 3:2). I will search for You in every place because without You I can do nothing, as You said: "For without Me you can do nothing" (Jn 15:5). If You are upset with me or angry at me, I will try to reconcile with You and apologize to You. I will not run away from You as my grandfather Adam did, for in You we "live and move and have our being" (Acts 17:28). As Your servant St. Paul said, "For to me, to live is Christ" (Phil 1:21). My soul is on her bed, but this is a temporary condition, which will end soon. It is incidental laziness; please do not consider it a lifetime characteristic.

It is true that I left You for a time, and ran after worldly pleasures, but they are simply pleasures, not love. True love belongs to You alone, total deep love. What binds me to the world are fleeting casual feelings, temporary pleasures that cannot rise to the level of love; love is an extremely deep emotion in the inner depths of the heart, which belongs to You and You to it.

To me, the world is transient, not the essence. As for true and eternal love, it is for You, and the heart belongs to You. You are the one whom my soul loves, even if I sometimes long for others. My soul cannot live if it does not find You; it cannot live without You. Likewise, as I seek You, You also seek me until You find me. And, when You find me, You will place me on Your shoulder rejoicing, as You did with the lost sheep when You found it: "And when he has found it, he lays it on his shoulders, rejoicing" (Lk 15:5).

Lord, You said, "If you love Me, keep My commandments" (Jn 14:15). I love You, but I have not yet kept Your commandments. I have not yet reached this level, and yet I do seek You, to give me the strength with which to keep Your commandments. Then I will love You by works and not only by feelings of the heart. It is true that I am in the night, but I am not far away from You. The darkness might surround me on the outside, but Your spirit continues illuminating my inside. I am in the dark night, but after this night there must be a dawn and a day. I am living in sin, apathy, and laziness, and yet I continue to seek the One my soul loves. This night does not bring despair, because it is not totally dark. Even if it were dark, You, O Lord, are able to illuminate it, because You are the true light. I fall into sin, and yet I do not love it, but rather, I love You. To me, sin is an external work, not internal. It is a weakness, a flaw, and it is neglect on my part. I commit it due to habit under external pressure. It can never be an expression of my hatred of You, O Lord!

No matter how much I sin and fall, I still love You, O Lord. I continue to seek You while on my bed. As for sin, I struggle to be rid of it. Sometimes I do not struggle, and yet, I wish with all my heart to be rid of it, along with all my weaknesses and sins. I would rejoice, O Lord, if You snatch me from it as "a brand plucked from the fire" (Zech 3:2). Then I would hear Your sweet chant: "Today salvation has come to this house" (Lk 19:9). I seek You with my whole heart. Whenever I sought You in my life and did not find You, even more did I seek You, because You are the only one that my soul loves. Whether I work in Your house, or if in laziness on my bed, my slumber on my bed is a temporary limited period of my life. It must end with the end of this night.

I am rebellious on this bed, and if I am unable to rise from it, You, O Lord, are able to raise me. I am currently lying on my bed, and the melody with which we start the psalmody is ringing in my ears: "Arise, O children of the Light, let us praise the Lord of Hosts."[28] Arise, O my soul, to meet "the one I love" (Song 3:3).

---

[28] 1990. *The Holy Psalmody*. Ridgewood: Saint Mary and Saint Antonios Coptic Orthodox Church, 2.

19. Lord, I Have Many Things to Say[29]

Lord, I have full trust in Your love for me, and that You can and want to seek my good. So why do I not confide in You as I confide in my beloved human friends? Do You see me finding pleasure while staying away from You, O Creator of all? Whenever You call me to You, I busy myself with other matters, and protest that my time is short.

Allow me, O Lord, to love You; teach me, O Lord, how to love You. Train me on Your love, and take me step by step in Your love. Pour Your love in my heart by the Holy Spirit.

Remove from my heart all other love that is incompatible with Your love, until the entire heart becomes for You alone. Do not allow me to love anything or anyone more than You, not even to love anyone, anything, or any desire that does not agree with Your love. O Lord, do not allow anyone or anything that competes with You to be found in my heart, or any that affronts Your love. Make Your love consume me and reign over my heart, leading all my actions, and blending perfectly with all my works, all my words, and with all my emotions. Give me, O Lord, the desire to sit and talk with You, to find pleasure in unceasing prayer.

---

[29] Excerpted from *Love, the Pinnacle of All Virtues.*

You, O Lord, have said, "I have this against you, that you have left your first love" (Rev 2:4), so, how can I return to my first love, except in You? It is You who restores me to Your love: "Restore me, and I will return, for You are the Lord my God" (Jer 31:18). It is You who gives me spiritual fervor, "for our God is a consuming fire" (Heb 12:29). Therefore, return me, O Lord, to my first love; rather, return me to even more.

20. YOU, O LORD, ARE COMPASSIONATE AND GENTLE[30]

*Y*ou, O Lord, the compassionate and gentle, the long suffering, how patient You have been with me while I was far away from You! How many opportunities have You given me to return to You! How much have You forgiven me, O Remitter, O Beloved; You did not treat me according to my sins! I, O Lord, I want to love You, but sin hinders my way to You and controls my heart and my love. I tried leaving it, but I could not.

Please give me the strength to leave it, for without You I cannot: "For without Me you can do nothing" (Jn 15:5). O Lord, save me from sinning, not in an attempt to escape punishment, but so that the obstacle preventing me from Your love is taken out of the way. Lord, please do not deprive me of Your love. Lord, share in the work with me, for without You, I can do nothing.

---

[30] Excerpted from *Love, the Pinnacle of All Virtues.*

21. LORD, I CANNOT FIND ANY BESIDES YOU[31]

O Lord, I have no family, clan, or land. You are my everything, and none compares. Since I met You, I no longer know anyone else. What is important to me, O Lord, is Your approval and blessing. I want to be reconciled with You, and reestablish Your dwelling in my heart. Escape from punishment is not what preoccupies me, but rather, Your love and fellowship. My ego is not important to me, but what is important is Your love. I seek reconciliation with You; after that, do with me as You please.

I, O Lord, have no strength; You have everything. It is You, O Lord, who protects me. Who can save himself? You are the one who keeps my soul. You keep it from all evil, from every slip, and from every temptation. You "deliver us from the evil one" (Mt 6:13; Lk 11:4); may You continue to keep us at all times. You protect us.

If You opened our eyes to see all that You have shielded us from, our entire lives would not suffice to thank You. Yours is the glory, Yours is the thanks, now and forever, Amen.

---

[31] Excerpted from *God and Man.*

22. Lord, of Your Own We Have Given You

$\mathcal{L}$ord, of Your own gifts, we have given You. It is You who give to us, and even further, it is You who give to those whom we seem to give. You also give us the love of giving.

Give me health and strength, to serve You with them. The more exhausted I am in Your service, no matter how much I exert in Your service, I will never consider that I have given You anything. Health is from You, strength is from You, and the love of service is also from You. Behold, I myself am from You. You gave me this existence with which to serve You. You also gave me the words to speak. In all my service to You, and my labor for You, I say, "Of Your own we have given You" (1 Chr 29:14).

These people, O Lord, need me to be constantly connected to You for them. Please allow me to be connected with You, not only for them, but also for myself, so that You care for me, and for them. Oh, that I become a useful bridge between them and You, or that I carry them in my heart to You.[32]

O Lord, until now, I have not offered You anything. Our father Abraham offered his only son, and the widow offered out of her need. What have I offered? Nothing.[33]

---

[32] Excerpted from *Spiritual Means.*
[33] Excerpted from *May the Lord Answer you.*

O Lord, I throw myself at Your feet. I do not claim any strength; I am weaker than weakness. I am too weak to fight even the smallest demons, and am no match for anyone. Support me, save me, and if one day I am victorious over any sin, I will say with all assurance, "The right hand of the Lord is exalted; the right hand of the Lord does valiantly" (Ps 118:16), and, "If it had not been the Lord who was on our side... then they would have swallowed us alive" (Ps 124:2-3).

The Lord Christ said to God the Father: "While I was with them in the world, I kept them in Your name. Those whom You gave Me I have kept; and none of them is lost" (Jn 17:12). Yes, You kept them. Not their strength, their piety, their cautiousness, their wisdom, their will and determination, nor even their love for You is what kept them; it was Your protection for them.

Give us strength, as You gave them, and lead us, as You led them in Your triumphal procession: "Now thanks be to God who always leads us in triumph in Christ" (2 Cor 2:14). When You held on to the hand of Peter, he was able to walk on the water with You, but through his own strength alone, he could not walk. He tried, and so fell in the water.

Keep us, O Lord, as You have kept them.[34]

---

[34] Excerpted from *Meditations on Great Friday*.

23. LET IT ALONE THIS YEAR ALSO[35]

*N*o, my Lord, no! Lift up Your ax slightly from the root of the tree. Let it alone this year also: "But he answered and said to him, 'Sir, let it alone this year also, until I dig around it and fertilize it'" (Lk 13:8). Give me another chance to repent.

Believe me, my Heavenly Father, though Your fatherhood is my greatest honor, it puts me to even more shame before my conscience. Whenever I tell You, "Our Father," I remember who I am, and who You are, O You who are in heaven, and my soul melts within me, being ground to dust and ashes. I call You Father, but I do not walk as Your son. Sonship requires resemblance between the son and his father, and I realize that I do not walk in Your likeness. I am not in Your image and likeness, for which You created me from the beginning. I do not act as befits the children of God. I fear that because of me, people might blaspheme Your Holy Name, "The name of God is blasphemed among the Gentiles because of you" (Rom 2:24). I wonder, would I dare and make a new request from You, to add, out of necessity, to this Lord's Prayer: "If You consent to calling me Your son, give me Your image, and give me the strength with which to act as Your son."

Are You not the one who said on the mouth of Your only-begotten Son: "Without Me, you can do

---

[35] Excerpted from *The Lord's Prayer.*

nothing" (Jn 15:5)? So, give me, O Lord, the ability to do Your work. Your saintly apostle says, "For it is God who works in you both to will and to do for His good pleasure" (Phil 2:13). Give me Your Holy Spirit who works in me, and works with me, so I may act as Your true son.

As You have given me Your name, as Your son, likewise, give me Your image. I am unable to attain it by my own effort alone; I receive Your image as a gratuitous gift from You. You gave me this divine image during baptism, when Your beloved Apostle stood to sing to me his beautiful chant, "For as many of you as were baptized into Christ have put on Christ" (Gal 3:27). Thus, I became a son to You, and an image of You; please keep me in this sonship and in this image.

24. LORD, YOU ARE BEYOND MY THOUGHTS[36]

*Y*ou, O Lord, are higher than my thoughts and my level of understanding. No matter how hard I try to understand Your height, I am unable to comprehend Your Essence and absolute Being. The simple mode, which I can understand as an unperceptive earthly human being, is that You are in heaven and that, despite Your height, You are willing to call me Your son and call Yourself my Father. Your name, O Lord, remains the same; it does not change. You are the Good Shepherd, and You are the compassionate Father, and You are the Guardian, the Keeper, the Helper, the Savior, the Loving, and the Compassionate, no matter how dark circumstances might seem before us. May Your name be hallowed in every mouth, in every heart and in every thought, regardless of the surrounding circumstances and the impression of some people.

Shall we say "The good shepherd" (Jn 10:11)? Or, O true Light: "That was the true Light which gives light to every man coming into the world" (Jn 1:9)? Or, "O You, the true Physician of our souls, and bodies, and spirits?"[37] Or, "O Holy Trinity, Father, Son and Holy Spirit": "In the name of the Father and of the Son and of the Holy Spirit... For there are three

---

[36] Excerpted from *The Lord's Prayer.*
[37] (H and H 2007), 344.

that bear witness in heaven: the Father, the Word, and the Holy Spirit; and these three are one" (Mt 28:19; 1 Jn 5:7)? Or, O heavenly King, or Pantocrator and Creator of all good? It is sufficient for us to chant "Your name is blessed and sweet in the mouths of Your saints."[38]

Due to the sweetness of Your name in our mouths, we want to constantly repeat it, because it gives joy to our hearts. Therefore, we chant, "Remembering Your Holy Name brings joy to our souls,"[39] as David the prophet said in the great Psalm: "How beloved is Your name, O Lord! It is my meditation the whole day."[40]

Just Your name, O Lord, is a consolation in afflictions. You are the heavenly King. May Your name be sanctified in every heart, thought, and understanding because it is the source of consolation and joy. Therefore, whenever a difficulty surrounds us, and we say, "O Lord," we are assured. Simply remembering Your name gives consolation, and so we call You, "O heavenly King." Whenever I remember Your name—Provider, Preserver, Helper, Protector, Pantocrator, Maker of all good, Lover of Mankind, Forgiver, Merciful—my heart is filled with solace, happiness, joy, and bliss, as we say, "The Bishop of all flesh, visit us with Your salvation."[41] Save us from all demons. This is why our fathers echoed Your holy

---

[38] (The Holy Psalmody 1990), 222.
[39] Ibid, 220.
[40] (Azmy 2009), 127 (Psalm 119:97).
[41] (H and H 2007), 344.

name thousands of times every day. We are in need, O Lord, for Your divine aid. This is why the psalmist said, "Unless the Lord builds the house, they labor in vain who build it; unless the Lord guards the city, the watchman stays awake in vain" (Ps 127:1). It is You who saves us, because we are unable to save ourselves.

25. YOUR KINGDOM COME[42]

*Y*ou, O Lord own us all, because You purchased us with Your precious blood, and because You created us out of nothing. You own this whole world, "The earth is the Lord's, and all its fullness, the world and those who dwell therein" (Ps 24:1).

If we say "Your kingdom come" (Lk 11:2), we will not have added to You something that is not Yours. This is Your own personal kingdom, which Satan wants to usurp from You. Please do not allow him this, for the glory of Your name. As long as the kingdom is Yours, let Your will prevail in Your kingdom, obeyed by all Your servants: "O God, unto whom every knee bows, those in the heavens, and those on earth."[43] In this, Your name will be hallowed. As long as the kingdom is Yours, You own the spiritual bread that You give us for our growth and for our eternal life. As long as the kingdom is Yours, You can issue a pardon to any guilty person in Your kingdom who begs Your mercy, who asks forgiveness, taking refuge in the blood which accomplished Your justice. As long as the kingdom is Yours, it befits Your Majesty to rescue us from the temptations that take us away from Your kingdom, and to save us from the evil one who resists Your kingdom and tries to attract

---

[42] Excerpted from *The Lord's Prayer.*
[43] (H and H 2007), 330.

us to another kingdom controlled by the unfruitful works of darkness.

We firmly believe that You have the power to reign, to make Your kingdom known. You have the power to carry out Your will. O Lord, it is sufficient for You to will; if You will, all things will be done by Your might. When we say, "Your will be done" (Lk 11:2), we mean for Your will to approve of our will, or better yet, for our will to agree with Your will. You have the power to work, to implement, and to respond. When we say "deliver us from the evil one" (Lk 11:4), we fully believe that You have the power to save us as You have saved our fathers. You also have the power with which to keep us from temptation. We ask of the God of powers, to whom, if He wills, nothing is difficult. We make all our requests to You, believing that Yours is the kingdom and the power; You are all encompassing.

We are overwhelmed, O Lord, by Your benevolence; Your graciousness to us is plentiful. Even if You do not give us anything now, Your past benevolence to us is enough; it is abundant.

26. BLESSED ARE YOU, O LORD[44]

O Lord, I do not deserve all this! Your grace, love, and gifts shame me. If You had treated me according to my merit, I would have been "counted with those who go down to the pit" (Ps 88:4).

Blessed are You, O Lord, in all Your love and Your protection. We ask You to be with us, as You were with Your disciples and Your saintly apostles with the same love, protection, and care. Indeed, Your prayers preserved Your disciples. Although they grew weak somewhat, their faith remained constant; it did not waver. This faith, which was in them, reached us through their evangelism. They were able, O Lord, to produce much fruit, as You commanded them: "God, who knows the heart, acknowledged them by giving them the Holy Spirit, just as He did to us" (Acts 15:8).

All this was through the blessings of Your Holy Passion, Your love for Your disciples, and Your strengthening them on Great Thursday. Then, You washed their feet, purified them, gave them Your body and blood, and sat with them, consoling and strengthening their faith.

Yours is the power, the glory, the blessing, and the majesty, forever, Amen.

---

[44] Excerpted from *The Prime Prayer and Psalm Fifty.*

27. Fulfill Your Promises to Us

$\mathcal{M}$y six days have been spent, in which I labored in the earth. Lord, You entered into Your Sabbath which never ends, of which the Holy Bible did not say, "So the evening and the morning were the seventh day!" My senses rested from all that occupied me in the world, and my relations with people became as a passenger glimpsing scenes through the portal of a speeding train![45]

Sufficient for us, O Lord, are the years of old eaten by the locusts (Cf. Joel 2:25). Sufficient are the lean years that passed by us unfruitful (Cf. Lk 13:7). There is no need for the old weaknesses to continue. We want to start a covenant with You, rejoicing in You and Your indwelling in our hearts, as You renew our youth like eagles (Is 40:31), and each one of us chants, "Restore to me the joy of Your salvation... Create in me a clean heart, O God, and renew a steadfast spirit within me" (Ps 51:12; 10:51). You absolutely will not allow, Lord, for the New Year to have the same weaknesses and lapses of last year. It is impossible for You to accept this, impossible! Then, give us strength to win.

We cling to Your promises which You mentioned in the book of Ezekiel the Prophet. You promised us, and You are faithful to Your promises. Fulfill Your promises to us. You told us on the mouth of Your

---

[45] Excerpted from *Experiences in Life II.*

servant Ezekiel, "I will give you a new heart" (Ezek 36:26). Where then is this new heart? You also said, "I will take the heart of stone out of your flesh" (Ezek 36:26). Until now, it has not been taken out, Lord. Cultivate this earth. As You have said in the days of old, "Let there be light... and saw the light, that it was good" (Gen 1:3-4), give this command once again, "show us Your mercy, Lord, and grant us Your salvation" (Ps 85:7). Give us this new heart and renew our minds: "Do not be conformed to this world, but be transformed by the renewing of your mind" (Rom 12:2).

I want, O Lord, to love You. I want Your love to dwell in my heart. I need to love goodness, holiness, virtue, and truth. I do not want to place before me goodness as a commandment, but as love. I do not want goodness to be a command that I struggle with myself to reach, but I want goodness to be love that I enjoy. I want Your commandments to be beloved by me so that I may find delight in them; I taste them, and they satisfy my soul. David the prophet said, "I will lift up my hands in Your name. My soul shall be satisfied as with marrow and fatness... Oh, how I love Your law! It is my meditation all the day... Therefore I love Your commandments more than gold, yes, than fine gold... How sweet are Your words to my taste, sweeter than honey to my mouth" (Ps 63:4-5; 119:97; 119:127, 103).[46]

---

[46] Excerpted from *Beginning a New Year.*

28. I WILL NOT LEAVE YOU[47]
(New Year's Eve)

Enter into my life and save me; I am as a man threatened with death. What should I do? I will cling onto the horns of the altar in the city of refuge, to find life, because if I let go of the horns of the altar, I will be led to death, having no strength. My heart loves You, or wants to love You, but still has a love for sin. I will not give You up for sin; I will strive to enjoy that verse that says: "I shall be whiter than snow," but I know I will not reach that until you wash me. Therefore, "Purge me with hyssop, and I shall be clean; wash me, and I shall be whiter than snow" (Ps 51:7).

Yes, this is what we say in church, in the prayers of the Divine Liturgy: "Purify our souls, our bodies, our spirits."[48] You are the one who purifies them, because they cannot be purified without You. You are the one who will purify our souls, bodies, and spirits, and grant us a new soul, a new spirit, a new heart. You will sprinkle us with pure water so that we are purified. You, O Lord, long ago, sprinkled me with pure water and purified me, but then I again contaminated myself. But I have hope in Your comforting words: "I will cleanse you from all your filthiness and from all your idols. I will give you a new

---

[47] Excerpted from *Beginning a New Year*.
[48] (H and H 2007), 223.

heart and put a new spirit within you" (Ezek 36:25-26).

Lord, purge me; I of myself am unable. If Your divine hand does not intervene to rescue and save, if Your Holy Spirit does not work within me, if You do not remove from me the heart of stone, if You do not sprinkle me with Your hyssop to purify me, and wash me to become whiter than snow, if You do not keep Your promises, I will not let You go this night. This entire past year, I will bury, O Lord, in Your plenteous mercies; I will toss it all in the abyss of Your love. I will leave it in the divine laundromat, where You wash my soul to become whiter than snow. I want nothing from that year. I relinquish it completely.

All I want, O Lord, is to start with You anew: "One thing I do, forgetting those things which are behind and reaching forward to those things which are ahead" (Phil 3:13). I want to start with You a new beginning, as You started in Your grace with Noah after You removed the entire ancient past and washed the earth from its impurities. This entire ancient past, I relinquish: "Sufficient for the day is its own trouble" (Mt 6:34). As for the New Year, I want to begin it with hope. "I will give you a new heart and put a new spirit within you" (Ezek 36:26). Where is this new heart, which You promised me, O Lord? And, where is this new spirit? Pardon me, O Lord, and forgive me, if I say, while under Your feet: "You owe me these promises. I will hold You to Your words. True, I am poor and needy, owning nothing, yet I hold Your promises. I hold Your love which You granted me freely. I hold Your covenant with me, and Your divine words: "I will cleanse you from all your filthiness and from all your idols… I will put My Spirit within you and cause you to walk in My statutes" (Ezek 36:25, 27). "Gird Your sword upon Your thigh, O Mighty One… draw it, prosper, and reign."[49] The work is not mine, but Yours.

Come, then, and reign. Personally remove the heart of stone and give me the new heart; grant me to submit to Your work in me, as a patient submits to the scalpel of the surgeon who cuts off what needs to be severed and joins up what needs connecting, unconscious and without volition. Let it be likewise with You, O Lord. Give me a new heart.

---

[49] (Azmy 2009), 44 (Ps 44:3-4).

29. YES LORD, YOURS IS THE POWER AND THE GLORY[50]
(On the prayers of Holy Pascha)

*Y*ou are He whom St. Paul described as "The power of God" (1 Cor 1:24). Those people assume that You are weak on the cross. As for us, we know who You are. Regarding Your power, we first know of Your power as the Creator: "All things were made through Him, and without Him nothing was made that was made" (Jn 1:3). Yours is the power as the Judge coming on the clouds of heaven to judge the living and the dead. Yes, this crucified, who appears weak before them, if they contemplated all the days that He spent among them on earth, they would have seen Him strong in everything. You, O Lord, are the only power that triumphed over sin, the world, and the devil. All humans were weak before sin, "for she has cast down many wounded, and all who were slain by her were strong men" (Prov 7:26). Therefore, the Holy Bible said, "They have all turned aside, they have together become corrupt; there is none who does good, no, not one" (Ps 14:3). But You, O Lord, You are the only one who challenged the world saying, "Which of you convicts Me of sin?" (Jn 8:46). Only You are strong enough to triumph over the devil and say, "The ruler of this world is coming, and he has nothing in Me" (Jn 14:30). Therefore, they sang to You in the Book of

---

[50] Excerpted from *Thine is the Power*.

Revelation, saying, "O Lord, holy and true" (Rev 6:10). You only are powerful in holiness, "holy, harmless, undefiled, separate from sinners, and has become higher than the heavens" (Heb 7:26).

O Lord, in Your miracles You demonstrated wondrous power, such that You had "done among them the works which no one else did" (Jn 15:24). You revealed Your power over nature, rebuking the wind, sea, and waves, and You walked over the waves of the sea. You are He to whom David sang, "You rule the raging of the sea; when its waves rise, You still them" (Ps 89:9). Yours is the power and the glory. You revealed Your power over disease and death; You healed "every sickness and every disease among the people" (Mt 9:35), especially incurable diseases. You healed the blind, the lepers, the bleeding woman, the man who had an infirmity for 38 years, the paralytic let down from the ceiling, and the man with the withered hand. You are the one who raised the dead, even the one who was in the tomb for four days and was said to have rotted.

You revealed Your power over creation. You revealed it in the miracle of feeding the thousands from five loaves and two fish, in the miracle of turning the water into wine (creating a new substance of a different element than water), and in creating eyes for the man born blind.

You revealed Your power over demons: "Demons also came out of many, crying out and saying, 'You are the Christ, the Son of God!'" If You rebuked a demon, it came out, unable to return. We cannot count Your miracles. Regarding them, what St. John the Beloved said is sufficient: "And there are also many other things that Jesus did, which if they were written one by one, I suppose that even the world itself could not contain the books that would be written" (Jn 21:25). These are various manifestations of the power of the Lord in His miracles.

When we glorify You, You do not increase. Rather, our mouths are sanctified by glorifying You. Honestly, when we glorify You, we do not give You glory, but we acknowledge Your glory. You, O Lord, are like the sun; it is luminous whether people acknowledge its light or not. Their admission of its light does not increase its brightness; it is self-luminous. We not only glorify You at Your awesome second coming, when Your glory will be clear, but we glorify You even in the depth of Your Passion.

We walk behind Your Passion step-by-step chanting: "Yours is the power and the glory, O Emmanuel, our God and King." We glorify You with this beautiful hymn, in which we tell You—in a wonderful immortal piece of music, music unparalleled in the world—"Your throne, O God, is forever and ever; a scepter of righteousness is the scepter of Your kingdom" (Ps 45:6)—Ⲡⲉⲕⲉ̀ⲑⲣⲟⲛⲟⲥ.[51]

---

[51] Here, His Holiness is referring to the famous Coptic Hymn PekEthronos (Your Throne) which is chanted on Pascha Tuesday and Great Friday.

In glorifying You, we are protesting against what the conspirators and crucifiers did to You. We protest what ungrateful humanity did to You. We see that Your true glory was in Your cross, which You endured for us. In glorifying You in Your crucifixion, we honorably accept the glory of the cross as life for us. Rather, we chant with the Apostle Paul, "I have been crucified with Christ; it is no longer I who live, but Christ lives in me" (Gal 2:20).

30. Chasten Me O Lord...What Son Is There whom a Father does Not Chasten?[52]

*C*hasten me, O Lord. "What son is there whom a father does not chasten?" (Heb 12:7). Those who do not accept chastening are illegitimate, not sons: "But if you are without chastening, of which all have become partakers, then you are illegitimate and not sons" (Heb 12:8). Chasten me, because chastening is beneficial for me; I deserve it. My sinful life deserves even stricter judgment, but please do not chasten me in Your hot displeasure, rather to a degree bearable to me. I accept Your chastening, O Lord, graciously. O Lord, consider me among those for whom You shed Your blood. "Have mercy on me, O Lord, for I am weak." I, O Lord, am weak before You, and weak before the devil who is "like a roaring lion, seeking whom he may devour" (1 Pt 5:8). My strength is in You: "The Lord is my strength and song, and He has become my salvation" (Ps 118:14). I am even weak before myself, and so, I continually ask Your assistance. I am weak before people, before "mighty men [who] have sought my soul; they have not set God before them,"[53] and so, have mercy on me, O Lord, for I am weak.

---

[52] Excerpted from *Do Not Rebuke Me in Your Anger*.
[53] (Azmy 2009), 53 (Ps 53:3).

31. TO YOU, O LORD, DO I COMPLAIN[54]

O Lord, O Lord, how can all this happen while You are watching and listening!

To You, O Lord, do I complain, and only You are able to console and strengthen me as You save me. You alone! As the saying goes, complaints to anyone other than God are humiliation. When I speak with You, I find comfort. I find comfort within me, reassured of Your work and intervention. I also find external comfort, as a result of Your work for me. You are the compassionate bosom on which I recline, and ask "Why?", or, "How can this happen?" "O Lord, those who afflict me have multiplied."[55] Certainly, O Lord, You are not one of them, because You are my consolation and salvation. Therefore, amid my troubles, I snatch up my flute to sing to You my psalms. Truly, "Is anyone cheerful? Let him sing psalms" (Jas 5:13). As for me, I sing to You in the depth of my troubles, because my delight is in You. I do not consider these troubles as discipline from You for me, but rather as a magnetic pull towards You.

As for my sin, You have forgiven it. If You feel that earthly punishments are beneficial for me, I accept them thankfully, but "deal gently… with the young man" (2 Sam 18:5). You, O Lord, with Your compassionate heart, will not leave me in my sins.

---

[54] Excerpted from *Lord How*.
[55] Cf. (Azmy 2009), 9 (Ps 3:1).

You are my shield. You are my conqueror. It is inevitable for You to lift me out of my fall, return me to my first rank, wash me to be whiter than snow, give me the joy of Your salvation, return and lift up my head, and return me to my first image so that I am glorified by You.

32. BLESSED ARE YOU, O LORD[56]

With all joy and tranquility I say, "Blessed are You, O Lord, in Your good promises, and in Your sincere faithful promise," that says "The Lord shall hear you in the day of your trouble."[57]

I, O Lord, will cling to Your word whenever I fall into trouble; I will use it when I reason with You. Have You not said, "Come now, and let us reason together" (Is 1:18)? So be it! You promised to answer in time of need, and Your promise is faithful and true. I stand by it, with all my faith, mind, and confidence in You, as God, the Lover of mankind, and as God, who keeps His promises. Give me, O Lord, this power with which to triumph. Please work in, and with me. As You conquered the world, conquer once more in my life. Are You not the One of whom it was said, "Behold, the Lion of the tribe of Judah, the Root of David, has prevailed" (Rev 5:5)? Conquer the world, and save me.

---

[56] Excerpted from *May the Lord Answer You.*
[57] (Azmy 2009), 36 (Ps 19:1).

33. YOU ARE LIFE ITSELF[58]

O Lord, I am unable to stay away from You for a single moment nor a twinkle of an eye. To me, You are life itself: "For to me, to live is Christ" (Phil 1:21). If I am separated from You, I am obsolete, and my life is worthless, the same as if I were dead, or nonexistent. My true existence is in You "that I may gain Christ and be found in Him" (Phil 3:8-9). I can never be separated from You. If I am separated at one point, know for certain that it is temporary, unnatural, and I do not desire it. Please return me to You by any means possible. Restore my soul, because without You, I will not live; in You I live, exist, and move, "for in

Him we live and move and have our being" (Acts 17:28). If I am detached from You, I become disconnected from power and grace, and become nothing. I return to dust, as I was, or rather, "like the chaff which the wind drives away" (Ps 1:4). O Lord, it is impossible for me to be isolated from You. "Restore my soul. Lead me in the paths of righteousness for Your name's sake" (Cf. Ps 23:3). Yours is the glory from now and forever, Amen.

---

[58] Excerpted from *Return to God.*

34. DO NOT DEPRIVE ME OF WORKING WITH YOU[59]

*L*ord, consider me among the despised and nonexistent, but do not deprive me of working with You. Allow me to have an existence before You, although, in my eyes, and perhaps in the eyes of people, I am despised and nonexistent (1 Cor 1:28).

O Lord, allow me to enter Your kingdom with the needy, the mutilated, the lame, and the blind. As You were careful to collect the fragments in the miracle of the five loaves and two fish, consider me among those fragments for Your apostles to take me with them in their baskets. I, O Lord, am of these fragments; gather me in Your blessed basket.

As long as Your promise, O Lord, stands before me, I will not fear the Red Sea if it blocks my path. You are able to split it, and pave a way for me through it, comforting me: "Walk in it and I am with you. I will keep you wherever you go." Even if Goliath were to stand before me, defying me all day long, threatening me with his spear which is like a weaver's beam, with his sword, strength, and self-satisfaction, I will answer him, "You come to me with a sword, with a spear, and with a javelin" (1 Sam 17:45), but the war is the Lord's. Therefore, I come to You with the divine promise: "Behold, I am with you and will keep you wherever you go" (Gen 28:15).

---

[59] Excerpted from *Life of Hope.*

35. YOU ARE INSIDE ME[60]

O Lord, it is a blessed hour when I sit with myself. When I sit with myself I sit with You, because, although I might not see You, You are within me. It is the same as when You were in the world and the world did not know You. O Lord, one of my biggest sins before monasticism was escaping from myself. I did not have time to sit with myself. Each time You freed me from preoccupations and concerns, to give me a chance to sit with myself, and sit with You, I—due to the abundance of my ignorance—looked for new engagements or concerns to occupy my time! I saw sitting with myself as a kind of slackness! In the world, I knew the theoretical importance of sitting with myself but, practically, I did not give any attention to this matter, or perhaps, the devil did not allow me to care for it. I was always busy; I had continuous uninterrupted engagements.

This is why, my Lord, I did not see the treasure found within me—You. When I used to sit and take some time to myself, and see even a slight ray of that treasure, I used to bury it for later. I used to hide it so as to "first go and bury my father" (Mt 8:21), see about my fields, or test my oxen (Lk 14:18-19)!

Finally, O Lord, when You allowed me on a certain day (I cannot recall exactly when) to sit with myself that long quiet session, and discover that treasure

---

[60] Excerpted from *Release of the Spirit.*

hidden within, I sold everything in exchange for that treasure—You. Behold, O Lord, I confess to You that now whenever I sit with myself, I feel every time that my *self* is more precious than the whole world, "For what will it profit a man if he gains the whole world, and loses his own soul?" (Mk 8:36). Whenever I feel that my *self* is more valuable than the world, the world grows smaller and smaller in my eyes, and I take from You the grace of indifference to everything. When I am thus indifferent, I find You before me, encouraging me: "Do not fear, for I am with you" (Gen 26:24).

When I sit, O Lord, with myself, I discover what is inside me, and I also see how the strangers transgressed Your sanctuaries within me (Jer 51:51). When I see that, and expose it before You, for You to keep my soul from strangers, then our session goes on and on, and I find many things to say to You. Here, human consolations pale in comparison. I do not seek human companionship, but rather I seek solitude, retreat, and stillness, so as not to be deprived of this dire need, my session with You, which provides me with contrition and purity. Sometimes, O Lord, when I sit with myself and dive deep within, I find serpents and scorpions lurking dormant in some corners, or trying to eat bits of my heart in silence or subtlety, and emit their toxins into my blood, my thoughts, and my feelings, unbeknownst to me.

When I see this, they awaken and try to bite my conscience, to trouble me. Too often I would rather leave it asleep so that it does not trouble me, but, what is the benefit, O Lord, for me to leave it thus, taking a step backwards, searching for self-consolation? It is a deception, an escape from the ego. Is it not better to uncover these snakes and combat them? Have mercy on me, O Lord, for I am weak, feeling my powerlessness to contend against their youngest. It is best to reveal them to You, O Lord, and for You to fight for me: "You will stretch out Your hand against the wrath of my enemies, and Your right hand will save me" (Ps 138:7).

When I sit, O Lord, with myself, I know the real me, and realize that I am dust and ashes before You, so my soul within me is humbled, and feels that worldly glory is but a false external coating that does not change a thing about the true self. When I sit with myself and feel my weakness, I cling to You ever more, sure that without You I can do nothing. The more I cling to You, the more You reveal Yourself to me, and I see that "You are more comely in beauty than the sons of men."[61] I love You, and love sitting with You more than sitting with other people. Each time I learn something new about You, so I become ever more drawn to You.

Give me, O Lord, to leave people, and become occupied with myself, to connect with You. Then, give me, O Lord, to forget myself, and be occupied only with You.

---

[61] (Azmy 2009), 44 (Ps 45:2).

36. I Want to Draw Closer to You[62]

O Lord, it is not I who go to You, because I do not know very well the way to reach You. My mind is limited, my spirit is trapped, I am bound to the body, and many other things keep me back, among them are my longings and desires, and yet, O Lord, sometimes I long to draw close to You! Furthermore, O Lord, I am distracted from You by many concerns that engage me. Due to the extent of my wretchedness and ignorance, I do not remove the false concerns, but rather add to them something new every day. Come to me, O Lord, reveal Yourself to me and visit me—as a son or as a slave—You who are full of love. Rather, You *are* love.

It is not I, O Lord, who build You a house in my heart to live in, because "unless the Lord builds the house, they labor in vain who build it" (Ps 127:1). Who am I that I should build You a holy temple for Your Holy Spirit to alight here? You, O Lord, built Jerusalem. Come, do not wait for me; You might wait long as I delay.

Not by my effort, O Lord, but by Your aid; not by my power, but by Your grace. I personally cannot understand, but You, through Your love, can reveal Yourself to me. You will not reveal Yourself to me unless I love You, but how can I love You if You do not reveal Yourself to me? Reveal Yourself to me, so

---

[62] Excerpted from *Release of the Spirit.*

that my love for You grows, and as I see new things in You, I will love You more and my relationship with You will grow. How can a person feel true love without knowing the recipient of his Love, without seeing Him, and only knowing vague details about Him?

Reveal Yourself to me, because this is the only means to truly know You—not through people or books—but through knowledge which we have seen with our eyes and our hands have handled (1 Jn 1:1).

I am unable to know You with perfect knowledge through books or through people who knew You, since those also cannot describe Your unutterable attributes; no tongue has the strength to speak of them. All they can do is entice the listener or reader by saying, "Come and see... Oh, taste and see that the Lord is good" (Jn 1:46; Ps 34:8), but, to manifest Your truth, they cannot!

But, if You revealed to me Yourself, O Lord... how can I see Your face, while, without holiness no one can see the Lord? Holiness is not within my means, "Lord, how they have increased who trouble me! Many are they who rise up against me" (Ps 3:1), and I am weak before them all: the world, the flesh, and the devil, weak before wants, desires, and thoughts. Too often I fall, and often I slip. Holiness is a dream I long for, but how can I reach it? Does this mean that I will not see You? Give me, O Lord, the purity of heart with which I can see Your face: "Purge me with hyssop, and I shall

be clean; wash me, and I shall be whiter than snow"
(Ps 51:7).

37. YOU, O LORD, EXIST[63]

*Y*ou, O Lord, exist. The vulnerable feel Your presence and are comforted, and if the powerful remembered Your existence, they would tremble.

Therefore, the expression "God exists" delights and terrifies, comforts and disturbs.

Yet, despite Your existence, many do not feel it. Therefore, Solomon cried out saying: "Then I returned and considered all the oppression that is done under the sun: And look! The tears of the oppressed, but they have no comforter" (Eccl 4:1). Why, O Lord, do You listen and remain silent? Show us, O Lord, Your mercy. Prove Your existence. Why do they reproach us saying: "Where is their God" (Ps 79:10)? Why do You wait until the last watch of the night, while the disciples in the ship are disturbed, and the waves are severe? Yes, why do You wait, while the Holy Bible says that You come and do not slacken (2 Pet 3:9)?

Hurry, Lord, hurry! David complained of this delay saying: "Make haste, O God, to deliver me! Make haste to help me, O Lord!... You are my help and my deliverer; O Lord, do not delay" (Ps 70:1, 5). We know that Your mercy will come, and that we are not to know the ages and times that You placed under Your authority, alone; therefore, we will wait

---

[63] Excerpted from *Release of the Spirit.*

unceasingly, as the psalmist said, "My soul has hoped in the Lord, from the morning watch till night."[64]

Here we are, Lord, waiting, believing that You exist, and that You must work. You will work mightily, wisely, and in the right time that Your unlimited compassion determines... How beautiful are the words of our Lord Jesus: "My Father has been working until now, and I have been working" (Jn 5:17). Work, Lord! Work for the sake of Your love of justice and righteousness. Work so that people are comforted and subsequently they will place their lives in Your hands, reflecting on Your work while silent, or reflecting on Your work while chanting that beautiful song: "The Lord will fight for you, and you shall hold your peace" (Ex 14:14). They will reflect on Your work, and will chant, while reassured, "God exists." Yes, indeed, God exists.

---

[64] (Azmy 2009), 98 (Ps 129:6).

38. I Thank You, O Lord

Thank You, Lord, for, had You seen a better situation for me than where I am, You would have taken me to there. Or, if I deserved more than this, You would have given me. Certainly, You always give me above what I deserve. It is enough that I trust Your wisdom and love in planning my life; this deserves thanks.[65]

O Lord, I never doubt Your love, no matter how many wounds I suffer, and whatever discipline I endure. It is all for good, and all for a blessing. "Your rod and Your staff, they comfort me" (Ps 23:4). If Your rod taps me, it is to lead and guide, and I do not feel any pain. You are the healing Discipliner, who injures and heals (Cf. Deut 32:39).

You did not intend pain for Job the righteous, but meant for him blessing through the pain, and brought him out of it better than he was: "Indeed the Lord gave Job twice as much as he had before... The Lord blessed the latter days of Job more than his beginning" (Job 42:10, 12). Job's words, "Blessed be the name of the Lord" (Job 1:21), were not when God healed him, but while in the depth of his trials and pains.[66]

---

[65] Excerpted from *Life of Thanksgiving.*
[66] Excerpted from *God and Man.*

39. HAVE MERCY ON ME

*W*e have nothing, O Lord, but Your mercy. We seek it from You in the evening, early morning, noon, and at all times, because You are the only one who has mercy, and You know our humiliation and misery, "For we are exceedingly filled with contempt" (Ps 123:3).[67]

Have mercy on me, O Lord, because if You do not have mercy on me, there is no one else who could have mercy on me. If Your heart is sealed, I will not find another. Your mercy is my blanket, my curtain. Your mercy is the basis of redemption, the basis of salvation.[68]

If the problems of our lives are because of weaknesses, please ease our lives, because You are stronger than our weaknesses. If there are obstacles in our lives, You, O Lord, are more powerful than all the obstacles.

---

[67] Excerpted from *Meditations in the Agpeya Prayers: The Vespers Prayer.*
[68] Excerpted from *O Lord Do Not Rebuke Me in Your Anger.*

40. I Want to Forget Myself

*W*ho am I, Lord, dust and ashes, that I should talk about myself and my requests during my prayers? I want to forget myself and remember You. I want to wade in Your unfathomable beauty, and Your unlimited perfection. I want to meditate on Your divine qualities which awe me such that I forget myself. When I forget myself, I will find myself in You, in Your massive, loving heart—this heart that I love from my depths. I long to live my whole life, and eternity also, musing in its love, care, forgiveness, tenderness, patience, and compassion for sinners "of whom I am chief" (1 Tim 1:15).

Who am I, O Lord, to stand before You—You before whom stand the angels, archangels, cherubim, seraphim, and all the innumerable powers of heavenly hosts? How can I squeeze myself among these luminous orders?[69]

I long for You, O Lord. I do not want to be away from You for any length of time.[70]

---

[69] Excerpted from *Spiritual Means*.
[70] Excerpted from *Spirituality of Fasting*.

41. I Want Nothing from the World[71]

I want nothing from the world, because I want You alone. You, who loved me until the end, and sacrificed Yourself for me. You, who created me when I was not. "You had no need of my servitude, but rather I had need of Your lordship."[72] I want to part from the world and unite with You, You who "have given to me the learning of Your knowledge."[73]

I want nothing from the world; I am not of the world...

All I want is to be rid of the world. I want to depart from it, from the body, from the dirt!

I want nothing from the world. I am looking for everlasting immortality. Nothing in the world remains forever, everything in it passes away; the world itself will pass away and perish. I am not searching for perishables.

I want nothing from the world. There is One from whom I ask, the rich, the powerful, in whom I find all my needs, being in want for nothing. He gives me before I ask of Him; He gives me what is beneficial and good for me.

Since I put myself in His hand, I no longer ask anything from the world.

---

[71] Excerpted from *Release of the Spirit*.
[72] (H and H 2007), 271.
[73] Ibid, 272.

42. I Finally Found You[74]

*F*inally, I have found You, O Lord, so, my heart was filled with joy, my tongue with praise, and my heart was filled with peace. Peace with You, since we have been reconciled, as long as You exist in me and I in You. First, may Your heart, O Lord, accept me, and after that do with me whatever You please. I have sinned against You, and I beg to reconcile with You that I may meet You and beg for forgiveness.

---

[74] Excerpted from *Return to God.*

POETRY

A Whisper of Love[75]

Throbbing heart of mine has Your resting place become
    In the inner recesses Your place have I concealed
I have left the world in all of its tumults
    And withdrawn from all, that I may with You live
No thought have I, nor opinion
    Nor other desire save to follow You
And Jacob my father's secret I perceive
    Now I know how he with You did wrestle
O heart's Companion, how sweet You are!
    High and Awesome, how splendid You are!
O Mighty One, in whose palm a whip
    Whilst love does Your tear-ducts bleed
The world cannot contain You, oh, how narrow it is!
    How, then, can the heart suffice to hold You in?
I have left the world in all of its tumults
    And withdrawn from all, that I may with You live

I have left all, my Lord, but You
    None have I in life's estrangement but You
And the mind have I checked from its wandering
    Wherever You are, there shall my thoughts be
Family and friends have I forgotten
    Nay, even the self, in the love of You
I have forgotten all in Your love
    O heart's Delight, forget not then Your son
Not distant are You from my spirit which in
    The stillness of silence does Your call await
In heaven You are indeed, yet every heart

---

[75] (Shenouda III 2020), 29.

89

Living in love, is for You a heaven
Your holy throne is a heart emptied
Of the love of all, and so loves none but You
Behold, the eye have I shut from beholding
That perhaps You I may behold
And the ear, too, have I emptied
That perhaps to You I may listen
Throbbing heart of mine has Your resting place become
In the inner recesses Your place have I concealed

Fr. Antonious Al-Souriany 1961
(His Holiness Pope Shenouda III)

I Love You, O Lord[76]

I love You, Lord, in my solitude
You call to my heart by Your words so deep
I love You, Lord, in tribulation
In my time of need, in my time of pain
I love You, Lord, in my repentance
In the time of tears, in the time of regret
I love You, Lord, in times prosperous
And I love You too in the time of scarcity
I love You as the palace is being built for me
And in its collapse, and in its destruction
I love You, the Heart Who my wound binds
And I rejoice when I see it healed
I love You, the Spirit Who hovers around me

Who grants my soul graces most sublime

His Holiness Pope Shenouda III 6/10/2008

Falling aground, he fractured his left femur.
Unaided for twelve hours, he decided:
"Will I let thoughts toss and turn in my head?
I will compose a poem!"

---

[76] (Shenouda III 2020), 38.

O My Lord [77]

O my Lord, my deepest love is Yours
O my Lord, I desire to see You
I desire to see You
In power, in glory, in majesty
Magnificent among Your heavenly hosts

Or to see You through the beauty of Your Son
Everyone who saw the Son, saw You
You're the fullness of the heart and the mind
I have no other but You in this sojourn

Among others, I draw them to You
In solitude, I'm inclined to call upon You:
Origin of the universe, O Creator
Your hands fashioned the earth in its glory

O my Lord, You are my strength and my fortress
You are my God, I live in Your protection
In You, my heart always is satisfied
My Lord, the joy of my heart is to please You

His Holiness Pope Shenouda III August 2008

---

[77] Contributed by blessed convent retreaters.

References

Azmy, Fr. Abraham, ed. 2009. *The Agpeya: The Coptic Prayer Book of the Seven Hours.* Hamden: Virgin Mary and Archangel Michael Coptic Orthodox Church.

H G Bishop Serapion, and H G Bishop Youssef. 2007. *The Divine Liturgies: The Anaphoras of Saints Basil, Gregory, and Cyril.* 2nd Edition. Dallas: Coptic Orthodox Diocese of the Southern United States.

His Holiness Shenouda III. 2020. *A Whisper of Love: Poems, Prayers, and Sayings.* Translated by Mary Bassilli and Amani Bassilli. www.Copticriches.com.

1990. *The Holy Psalmody.* Ridgewood: Saint Mary and Saint Antonios Coptic Orthodox Church.

The Douay-Rheims American Edition. 1899.

The New King James Version. Nashville: Thomas Nelson, Inc, 1982.